COUNTRY

Formal Name: Malaysia.

Short Form: Malaysia.

Term for Citizen(s): Malaysian(s).

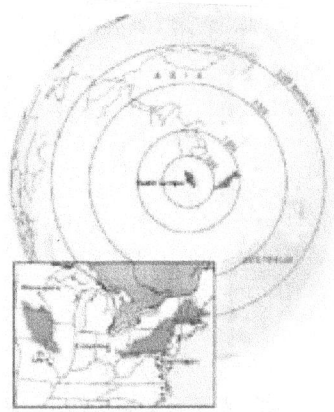

Capital: Since 1999 Putrajaya (25 kilometers south of Kuala Lumpur) has been the administrative capital and seat of government. Parliament still meets in Kuala Lumpur, but most ministries are located in Putrajaya.

Major Cities: Kuala Lumpur is the only city with a population greater than 1 million persons (1,305,792 according to the most recent census in 2000). Other major cities include Johor Bahru (642,944), Ipoh (536,832), and Klang (626,699).

Independence: Peninsular Malaysia attained independence as the Federation of Malaya on August 31, 1957. Later, two states on the island of Borneo—Sabah and Sarawak—joined the federation to form Malaysia on September 16, 1963.

Public Holidays: Many public holidays are observed only in particular states, and the dates of Hindu and Islamic holidays vary because they are based on lunar calendars. The following holidays are observed nationwide: Hari Raya Haji (Feast of the Sacrifice, movable date); Chinese New Year (movable set of three days in January and February); Muharram (Islamic New Year, movable date); Mouloud (Prophet Muhammad's Birthday, movable date); Labour Day (May 1); Vesak Day (movable date in May); Official Birthday of His Majesty the Yang di-Pertuan Agong (June 5); National Day (August 31); Deepavali (Diwali, movable set of five days in October and November); Hari Raya Puasa (end of Ramadan, movable date); and Christmas Day (December 25).

Flag: Fourteen alternating red and white horizontal stripes of equal width, representing equal membership in the Federation of Malaysia, which is composed of 13 states and the federal government. In the upper left quadrant, a yellow crescent and star, which represent Islam, are centered in a solid blue rectangle.

HISTORICAL BACKGROUND

Early History to the Fourteenth Century: Little is known about Malaysia's early history, but historians believe that as early as the first few centuries A.D. trade on the Strait of Malacca helped to create economic and cultural links among China, India, and the Middle East. Among the most powerful and enduring early kingdoms was Srivijaya, which ruled much of Peninsular Malaysia from the seventh to the fourteenth century with support from China and the Orang Laut ("men of the sea") who originated from Peninsular Malaysia and were perhaps the region's best sailors and fighters. By the fourteenth century, Srivijaya's dominance had ended because it lost Chinese support and because it was continually in conflict with states seeking to dominate lucrative trade routes. As for the other region of Malaysia, Borneo, evidence suggests that Borneo developed quite separately from the peninsula and was little affected by cultural and political developments there. The kingdom of Brunei was Borneo's most prominent political force and remained so until nineteenth-century British colonization.

The Malacca Sultanate and the Evolution of Malay Identity: The commencement of the current Malay nation is often traced to the fifteenth-century establishment of Malacca (Melaka) on the peninsula's west coast. Malacca's founding is credited to the Srivijayan prince Sri Paramesvara, who fled his kingdom to avoid domination by rulers of the Majapahit kingdom. By the late fourteenth century, Malacca had become an important commercial power and cultural influence along the Strait of Malacca, largely as a result of its numerous advantages as a trading port and its commercial and military alliances with China and the Malay kingdom of Bintan, an island near Singapore and home of the Orang Laut. When Muzaffar Shah became Malacca's ruler in 1444, he declared the kingdom a Muslim state, and Malacca's growing commercial, military, and political influence helped spread the Islamic faith throughout the region.

European Intrusion and the Fall of Malacca: Near the beginning of the sixteenth century, European powers became interested in Malacca's trade and the opportunity to spread Christianity in Asia. In 1511 Portugal conquered Malacca, but Portuguese efforts to establish a trade monopoly were thwarted by military raids conducted by Malacca's ruler Mahmud Shah and by his sons' kingdoms, particularly Johor. Throughout the sixteenth century, Portugal, Johor, and Aceh (in Indonesia) variously fought and allied with one another in order to establish a trade monopoly in the region. By 1641, the Dutch had entered the fray, and an alliance with Johor helped the Dutch defeat the Portuguese and assume control of Malacca.

The Malay States to the End of the Eighteenth Century: In the eighteenth century, various struggles for political and economic influence fragmented authority in the Malay world, so that conflict and instability were the norm. In the peninsula's western areas, two groups that had migrated to the peninsula for centuries, the Buginese and the Minangkabau, often fought each other. By 1740 the victorious Buginese ruled many peninsular states and continued to do so until they were defeated by an alliance of Johor and the Dutch in 1784. In eastern areas of the peninsula, Thai kingdoms often fought with and ruled Malay kingdoms from the sixteenth to the eighteenth centuries. Furthermore, Malay waters become some of the most dangerous in the world. Dutch monopolistic trade practices encouraged substantial black-market trade, and idle *anak raja* (sons of rulers) supported piracy as a means of income and recreation suitable to their elite status. Similarly, in Borneo piracy and slave raids supported by foreign powers were common. Piracy even forced the British East India Company to abandon two island settlements (in 1775 and 1776) off the coast of Borneo.

The British Colonial Presence: The British presence was minimal in the Malay world until 1785, when a former British naval officer and private trader, Francis Light, acquired for the British a grant to the island of Penang from the sultan of Kedah. In 1786 Light established the settlement of George Town on Penang, and within a few years the island's free-trade policy helped it eclipse Malacca as the peninsula's premier trade center. The British presence on the Malay Peninsula expanded in 1819 when Thomas Stanford Raffles, a British East India Company official, and Tunku Hussain, a contender for the throne of Malacca, agreed that the British could settle in Singapore in exchange for formal recognition of Hussain as Malacca's sultan. Singapore soon became an astonishing financial success because of its advantageous geographic location and its free-trade policies.

British influence expanded further with the Anglo-Dutch Treaty of 1824, which effectively split the Malay world into territories that would become Indonesia and Malaysia. By 1826 the British had joined the peninsular territories of Malacca, Penang, Perai (then known as Province Wellesley), Dindings (now part of the state of Perak), and Singapore under a single administration called the "Straits Settlements."

Federated and Unfederated Malay States: The British were reluctant to acquire other commitments in the region, but periodic forays by Siam (now Thailand) into north Malay states, piracy supported by Malay rulers, and periodic conflicts between Malay rulers of tin-producing states and Chinese tin miners mobilized by Chinese secret societies all threatened British commercial interests and prompted the British to become increasingly involved in peninsular affairs. In the 1870s, the British adopted a system of indirect rule over Malay states that furnished the beginnings of a centralized state. In 1874 the British agreed to recognize and support a contender as the sultan of Pangkor in exchange for the sultan's acceptance of a British representative, or "resident," whose advice would be sought and followed on all issues except Malay custom and religion. British residents were later established in three other tin-producing states, which became known as "protected states." In 1896 the Malay rulers of these states and Pangkor signed the Treaty of Federation, which established the Federated Malay States. Malay rulers were invited to provide input into the federation's development, but in reality the new constitutional arrangements were designed to provide an appearance of Malay rule while effectively reducing traditional rulers to mere decorous bystanders.

A different governing arrangement was established with other Malay states that were more independent of British control than the Federated Malay States. Siam tenuously controlled the northern states of Kedah, Terengganu, Kelantan, and Perlis until a 1909 treaty between Britain and Siam placed those states under British influence. The sultans of these states refused to join the federation, but they did accept British advisers. Unlike residents, the advisers had no effective executive power and relied on diplomacy with the sultans for policy matters. The southern state of Johor also remained relatively independent of British influence until 1909, when the sultan accepted a British "financial adviser" with wide-ranging powers. Thus, by 1914 the Malay Peninsula was composed of 10 political entities: the Straits Settlements, four Federated Malay States, and five Unfederated Malay States.

Borneo in the Nineteenth Century: From the sixteenth to the early nineteenth centuries, developments in Borneo were generally separate from those on the peninsula, partly because of more limited European involvement in Borneo. That situation changed in 1839 when James Brooke, an independently wealthy former British East India Company officer, arrived in Borneo and helped the sultan of Brunei to emerge victorious in a power struggle with other Brunei elites. In return, the sultan allowed Brooke to govern a territory (called Sarawak) in exchange for small annual payments. Through good relations and payments to the Brunei sultan, Brooke and his descendents expanded Sarawak's territory and governed with substantial autonomy from Britain. Eventually, the British government became concerned that Sarawak's growth could destabilize Brunei and render Borneo vulnerable to seizure by rival powers. In 1888 the British agreed to provide protection to Sarawak, Brunei, and the British North Borneo Company (which administered the territory of Sabah) in exchange for control over their foreign policy. This contributed to the consolidation of northern Borneo and its separation from the island's southern areas, which were governed by the Dutch.

Early Twentieth Century: By the late nineteenth century, stable forms of government had emerged in Malaysia, and its economy and culture began to assume characteristics that would endure for decades. In the late 1800s, copious deposits of tin ore were discovered in the northwestern state of Perak, and this led to substantial growth in mining and the creation of administrative and transportation infrastructure to service the tin industry, which in turn enabled the growth of other industries along the west coast, such as rubber plantations. This early export diversification helped the economy respond to changing international prices for primary commodities and generally aided economic growth.

In addition, an ethnic Malay identity began to emerge in this period. Although ethnic Malays shared a common religion in Islam and a common language in Malay, their social identities were often localized to their respective states, and their political loyalties were generally to their respective sultans. By contrast, the Chinese and Indians in Malaysia often occupied particular economic niches, which helped instill in them more distinct and salient ethnic identities. This situation began to change in the early 1900s with the emergence of Malay cultural organizations and publications. These entities had numerous political differences but generally claimed that Malays share a common ethnicity and thus promoted the emergence of the Malay nation.

War, Emergency, and Independence: Japanese forces attacked Singapore on December 10, 1941, and by February 15, 1942, the Japanese occupied the Malay Peninsula and Singapore. Under Japanese occupation, ethnic tensions between Malays and Chinese crystallized because Malays filled many administrative positions while the Chinese were treated harshly for their resistance activities and for supporting China's war of resistance against the Japanese in the 1930s. When the British resumed control in 1945, they sought to establish themselves as a durable administrative power, and ethnic tensions often influenced political arrangements. In January 1946, the British proposed the Malayan Union plan, which would make Singapore one colony and create another colony from the previously separate Federated and Unfederated Malay States, Penang, and Malacca. Naturalization requirements would be eased for non-Malays. But fearing that they would become a minority group in the new state, many ethnic Malays opposed this plan, including Malaysia's first political party, the United Malays National Organization (UMNO), which was formed in March 1946. Despite Malay opposition, the British implemented the Malayan Union on April 1, 1946, but they soon considered amending it because its support by the largely ethnic Chinese Communist Party of Malaya (CPM) led to fears of potential communist influence. In May 1947, the British proposed maintaining the same territorial arrangement but as a majority-Malay federation that would have greater autonomy on matters such as Malay customs and religion. Ethnic Chinese and Indians were uneasy about living under an ethnic Malay majority, and left-wing Malay and Chinese groups organized strikes against the new proposal. However, the Federation of Malaya Agreement was implemented on February 1, 1948.

Civil conflict soon followed, and the British government declared a state of emergency on June 18, 1948. The CPM's armed division, the Malayan Races Liberation Army (MRLA), engaged in a rural insurgency, but the insurgents were poorly organized and had little success after 1951. The British were able to undermine MRLA support by moving ethnic Chinese out of rural squatter areas and into government-controlled "New Villages" that were equipped with better health and educational facilities than in squatter areas. The MRLA was eventually forced into areas bordering Thailand, and by 1960 the "Emergency" was formally declared at an end.

The Alliance and Independence: In the 1948 Federation of Malaya Agreement, the British agreed to grant eventual self-rule, but ethnic tensions were a major obstacle to doing so. The British tried to promote national unity among different ethnic groups by encouraging dialogue among noncommunist ethnic leaders, but the eventual consensus was that Malays would only share political power with non-Malays if non-Malays helped improve Malays' economic status. The details to implement this plan remained elusive, and the groups engaged in discussions were largely ethnically based: UMNO, the Malaysian Chinese Association (MCA), and the Malayan Indian Congress (MIC). However, from 1952 to 1955 UMNO, the MCA, and the MIC established a partnership called the "Alliance" that won municipal, local, and federal elections and thus emerged as an agent for unified Malayan interests. By October 1956, a Constitutional Commission had produced a document that included numerous compromises to satisfy the various ethnic, religious, and linguistic concerns of Malaya's diverse population. For example, Malay was proclaimed the national language, but English would continue as a national language for at least 10 years. Islam became the official state religion, but religious freedom for all religious groups was guaranteed. Malays retained various special privileges, but non-Malay rights could not be hindered by prejudicial legislation or governmental intervention. On August 15, 1957, the Federal Legislature ratified the document, and on August 31, 1957, Malaya became an independent country.

The Creation of Malaysia: Singapore requested inclusion in the Federation of Malaya in 1957 and again in 1959, but Malay leaders were uneasy about Singapore's leftist politics and feared that the addition of Singapore would make Malaya a majority-Chinese state. In order to overcome such concerns, Singapore and Malaya met with the British and proposed an association that would include Brunei, Malaya, North Borneo (Sabah), Sarawak, and Singapore. The proposal generally neutralized Malay opposition because the projected federation's states would all have indigenous majorities, but some groups in North Borneo, Sarawak, and Singapore opposed this proposal. Nevertheless, in 1962 and 1963 pro-merger political parties won elections in all of these territories. The 1957 constitution was amended to include numerous compromises among the states, and on September 16, 1963, the Federation of Malaysia came into existence. Brunei's sultan, however, opted to remain independent since he was reluctant to be only one of 10 Malay rulers or to share Brunei's oil revenues.

External Threats: "Confrontation" and the Philippine Claim to Sabah: Newly independent Malaysia was soon faced with external threats from Indonesia and the Philippines. The Indonesian government led by Sukarno contended that the new federation was a neocolonialist plan to prevent Indonesia and Malaysia from combining into a Greater Malaysia, an entity that Malaysian leaders had previously supported. Soon after the Federation of Malaysia was established, Indonesia attempted to spark a popular revolt in the fledgling country by engaging in acts of terrorism and armed confrontation in various places. However, these actions strengthened popular support for Malaysia, and in 1964 Australia, Britain, and New Zealand sent troops and military aid to Malaysia. An abortive coup attempt in 1965 forced Sukarno to step down, and on August 11, 1966, Indonesia and Malaysia signed a peace treaty. The Philippines' differences with Malaysia did not involve organized violence but were longer lasting. A legally complex territorial dispute over Sabah led to the occasional suspension of diplomatic relations between 1963 and 1968, although relations were restored in December 1969. Relations were later strained as Sabah's chief minister allowed Muslim insurgents from the Philippines to use Sabah as a haven until he lost an election in April 1976.

The Secession of Singapore: Malaysia's independence was also followed by difficulties with Singapore. Under the terms of federation, Singapore accepted underrepresentation in the House of Representatives and also accepted that its residents could not participate as full citizens in Malaysia without fulfilling stringent naturalization requirements. Singapore's chief minister Lee Kwan-Yew was, however, critical of Malays' special status, and Malays perceived Lee's efforts to reduce their special status as an attack on Malay rights and on the country's racial harmony. In August 1965, officials from the federal government and Singapore held secret meetings to arrange for Singapore's peaceful withdrawal from Malaysia, and Singapore became independent on August 6, 1965.

The Kuala Lumpur Riots of May 1969 and Their Aftermath: After the separation of Singapore and Malaysia, ethnic issues continued to simmer between Malays and Chinese. In the elections of May 1969, the Alliance was opposed by the Democratic Action Party, which had a predominantly Chinese following and advocated the abolition of Malays' special status. After a bitter campaign between the two sides, the Alliance maintained power but lost a significant share of the total vote. Opposition party supporters held public demonstrations to celebrate their election gains, and violence broke out between opposition supporters and Malay bystanders. Riots ensued for two weeks, mostly in Kuala Lumpur, and resulted in hundreds of casualties, primarily Chinese and Indians. The government declared a state of emergency and ultimately passed laws against questioning governing institutions and Malays' special status.

In 1972 UMNO created a partnership with the Pan-Malaysia Islamic Party (PAS) to reduce intra-Malay political differences and also renewed ties with the MCA, which had left the Alliance prior to the Kuala Lumpur riots. This broader, interracial coalition changed its moniker to the National Front (Barisan Nasional—BN) and won large majorities in the 1974 federal and state elections. Throughout the 1970s and 1980s, BN administrations succeeded in increasing the power of the federal government relative to the state governments, often by forcing out of office independent-minded state chief ministers who were perceived as presenting a threat to national unity and ethnic accord. The BN also promoted educational policies designed for ethnic Malays and adopted aggressive measures to address economic inequalities experienced by Malays.

Mahathir and the Growth of Malaysia: In 1981 Mahathir Mohamad became prime minister, which caused concern among ethnic Chinese and Indians in Malaysia who regarded him as interested in promoting Malay status at the expense of other ethnic groups. However, Mahathir's early years in office were marked primarily by attempts to prevent official corruption and by success in increasing the power of elected officials relative to Malay rulers. Mahathir also ambitiously pursued economic reforms, such as orienting the economy toward the production of export goods, promoting joint ventures with Asian firms, and privatizing many state industries, which often were taken over by ethnic Malay-controlled corporations.

Mahathir's economic and other policies were subject to widespread criticism, which occasionally led to contentious divisions within UMNO. He was often viewed as uncompromising and highly aggressive in the pursuit of his policies, yet throughout the 1980s he led UMNO and the BN to successive election victories. Heightened criticisms of Mahathir coincided with rising ethnic tensions over religion, Chinese-language education, and other issues. Claiming to preempt violent ethnic riots, in 1987 Mahathir ordered a crackdown on critics of government policies, and police arrested more than 100 individuals—including politicians—and closed three newspapers. The detainees were later released, but the government introduced numerous restrictions on civil liberties, such as making the dissemination of "false" news illegal.

In the 1990s, UMNO and the BN continued their impressive streak of election victories, and Mahathir's influence continued to grow. However, by the late 1990s long-simmering tensions between Mahathir and Minister of Finance Anwar Ibrahim led to one of Malaysia's most controversial political episodes. In 1993 Anwar won UMNO's internal election for deputy president against Mahathir's close ally Ghafar Baba and thus became Malaysia's deputy prime minister and, in the eyes of some observers, a potential rival to Mahathir. In May 1997, Mahathir took a two-month leave of absence and appointed Anwar acting prime minister. In July 1997, many Asian countries were plunged into an economic crisis, and Mahathir severely criticized international investors for precipitating the crisis. By contrast, Anwar gained political favor by attempting to reassure investors with various free-market reforms, many of which financially threatened banks and infrastructure projects favored by Mahathir and some of his associates. In 1998 Anwar was arrested and eventually prosecuted for alleged sodomy and corruption, although many observers suggested that these developments were politically motivated. In 2004 the sodomy charged was overturned, and Anwar was released from prison.

In January 1999, Mahathir engaged in a major reshuffling of his cabinet, and the most significant change was that Abdullah Ahmad Badawi was appointed as deputy prime minister and minister for home affairs. In November 1999, the BN coalition won a decisive victory in national elections. The following month, Mahathir announced that he would not run again for office and officially declared Abdullah as his chosen successor. Mahathir retired in October 2003 and was succeeded by Abdullah, who subsequently pursued policies that were often at odds with Mahathir's previous policies. Whereas Mahathir was criticized for corruption and cronyism, Abdullah has engaged in substantial anticorruption efforts and terminated many government-funded projects that were administered by Mahathir's associates. These changes and continuing ethnic tensions led many to question how long Abdullah would be politically influential, but the BN coalition won general elections held in March 2004, and Abdullah was elected as UMNO party president. Furthermore, Abdullah has continued Malaysia's impressive emergence from the 1997 economic crisis and its economic growth.

GEOGRAPHY

Click to Enlarge Image

Location: Malaysia is located in Southeast Asia. Most of it land area is contained in two noncontiguous regions separated by about 530 kilometers of the South China Sea. One region is Peninsular Malaysia, which is bordered by Thailand to the north, the Strait of Malacca to the west, the Johore Strait to the south, and the South China Sea to the east. The other region, sometimes called East Malaysia, is the northern portion of the island of Borneo that is composed of two states, Sabah and Sarawak. The Kingdom of Brunei and the Indonesian territory of Kalimantan make up the rest of Borneo. Malaysia also encompasses many small islands, the largest of which is Labuan, off the coast of Sabah.

Size: Malaysia's total land area is 329,758 square kilometers: 131,598 square kilometers in Peninsular Malaysia and 198,160 square kilometers in Sabah and Sarawak.

Land Boundaries: Malaysia's land boundaries total 2,669 kilometers. There is one land boundary on the peninsula, a 506-kilometer border with Thailand. On Borneo, Malaysia has a 381-kilometer border with Brunei and a 1,782-kilometer border with Indonesia.

Disputed Territory: Malaysia has several territorial disputes with other countries, but none have resulted in military conflict. Malaysia disputes sovereignty over the possibly oil-rich Spratly Islands with Brunei, China, the Philippines, Taiwan, and Vietnam. The Philippines previously claimed the state of Sabah, and Indonesia has disputed Malaysia's incorporation of Sarawak. However, both claims appear dormant. Indonesia and the Philippines claim the Ligitan and Sipadan Islands, which the International Court of Justice (ICJ) awarded to Malaysia in 2002. However, the ICJ left those islands' maritime boundaries in the hydrocarbon-rich Celebes/Sulawesi Sea unsettled, and thus the countries still have overlapping claims to petroleum resources located in the seabed. Brunei and Malaysia both claim offshore seabeds, so the dispute has terminated gas and oil exploration in the area. Finally, Malaysia has disputed Singapore's land reclamation, bridge construction, maritime boundaries, and claim to Pedra Branca Island (Pulau Batu Putih), approximately 15 kilometers off the southern coast of the state of Johor. However, in 1998 the two countries agreed to future ICJ arbitration on the island dispute, and observers expect the case will be heard in 2007.

Length of Coastline: Malaysia's total coastline is 4,675 kilometers in length: 2,068 kilometers for Peninsular Malaysia and 2,607 kilometers for East Malaysia.

Topography: The topography of Peninsular Malaysia, Sabah, and Sarawak is generally coastal plains with hills and mountains in the interior. Malaysia's lowest elevation is sea level along the coasts, and the highest is Gunung Kinabalu in northern Sabah at 4,100 meters. In 2005 forests covered approximately 64 percent of the country's total land area.

Principal Rivers: Malaysia's principal rivers are the Kinabatangan (564 kilometers in length), Rajang (560 kilometers), Pahang (434 kilometers), Baram (400 kilometers), Lupar (230 kilometers), and Limbang (196 kilometers).

Climate: Peninsular Malaysia and East Malaysia, both just north of the equator, are subject to the same movement of air masses and have similar climates. Temperatures and precipitation vary by elevation and proximity to the sea, but temperatures tend to be uniform year-round with annual average temperatures ranging from 23° C to 34° C. Rainfall is heavy with annual southwest monsoons from April to October and northeast monsoons from October to February. Total annual rainfall ranges from 1,300 to 4,700 millimeters in East Malaysia and from 1,400 to 4,000 millimeters on the peninsula. Humidity is also high; mean relative humidity ranges from 80 to 90 percent.

Natural Resources: Malaysia's most economically significant natural resource is tin; its tin deposits are the most extensive in the world. Other important natural resources are bauxite, copper, gold, iron ore, natural gas, petroleum, and timber.

Land Use: According to an estimate from 2001, 5.5 percent of Malaysia's land is categorized as arable, 17.6 percent is covered by permanent crops, and the remaining 76.9 percent categorized as "other." Cleared land exists only in major settlement areas along the coast or on the banks of rivers for differing distances inland. Much cleared land has been used for palm and rubber tree plantations.

Environmental Factors: Malaysia faces many natural hazards, particularly flooding, landslides, and forest fires. Human-induced transformation of the environment is often regarded as more problematic than natural disasters but less so than in other Asian countries. Automobile emissions are Malaysia's major source of air pollution, but air quality indicators for Malaysian cities tend to indicate cleaner air than in most other Asian cities. Livestock farming, domestic sewage, and landclearing have contributed to river pollution, but government documents do not suggest that river pollution is widespread or acutely problematic. Oil and grease have polluted coastal waters in all states and groundwater in some areas, and rates of deforestation increased from 0.4 percent annually during the 1990s to 0.7 percent annually from 2000 to 2005.

Time Zone: Malaysia is eight hours ahead of Greenwich Mean Time (GMT).

SOCIETY

Population: From 1960 to the most recent census in 2000, the total population grew from an estimated 8 million to 23.3 million persons. The annual population growth rate averaged 2.6 percent for that period, gradually declining to 1.8 percent for 2005–6. Government figures for the first quarter of 2006 put the total population at 26.5 million. In 2000 the state with the highest population was Selangor (4.2 million), and Labuan had the lowest population (76,067). Total population figures include approximately 1.4 million non-Malaysian citizens, who comprised 5.9 percent of the total population in 2000. From 1960 to 2000, population density grew from 24 to 71 persons per square kilometer. In 2000 population density was lowest in the state of Sarawak

(17 persons per square kilometer) and highest in the federal region of Kuala Lumpur (5,676 persons per square kilometer). From 1960 to 2000, the percentage of the population residing in urban areas increased from 25 to 62 percent.

Demography: According to the 2000 census, 50.9 percent of the population was male and 49.1 percent female. Furthermore, 33.3 percent of the population was less than 15 years of age, 62.8 percent was 15 to 59 years of age, and 3.9 percent was 65 years of age or older. According to government data, from 1980 to 2005 life expectancy at birth increased from 66.4 to 71.8 years for males and from 70.5 to 76.2 years for females. During the same period, the crude birthrate fell from 30.9 to 19.6 births per 1,000 persons, the crude death rate fell from 5.3 to 4.4 deaths per 1,000 persons, and the infant mortality rate fell from approximately 23.9 to 5.1 deaths under one year of age per 1,000 live births. However, these figures often vary among ethnic groups.

Ethnic Groups: According to the 2000 census, 50.2 percent of the population is Malay, 24.5 percent Chinese, 11 percent indigenous, 7.2 percent Indian, and 1.2 percent members of other ethnic groups. Non-Malaysian citizens make up the remaining 5.9 percent. These groups often can be divided by language, tribe, and other categories. Since independence, a common national identity has solidified, but ethnic divisions remain apparent in many aspects of daily life. Malays and indigenous groups often refer to themselves as *bumiputra* ("sons of the soil"), and ethnicity is associated with differences in politics, residence, socioeconomic position, and daily customs. The government has affirmative-action policies designed to promote social harmony, but critics claim such policies unfairly favor ethnic Malays over other groups.

Languages: Bahasa Melayu is the official language. Other commonly spoken languages include English, Tamil, Telugu, Malayalam, Panjabi, Thai, and various dialects of Chinese (Cantonese, Mandarin, Hokkien, Hakka, and Hainan). In Eastern Malaysia, several indigenous languages are spoken, but Iban and Kadazan are the most prominent. The Malaysian census does not maintain data for the population of linguistic groups, but language and ethnicity are strongly associated.

Religion: Islam is the official religion, but freedom of religion is constitutionally guaranteed. According to government statistics, in 2000 approximately 60.4 percent of the population was Muslim, and Muslims were the highest percentage in every state except Sarawak, which was 42.6 percent Christian. Buddhism was the second most adhered to faith, claiming 19.2 percent of the population, and Buddhists constituted at least 20 percent of the total population in many states of Peninsular Malaysia. Of the remaining population, 9.1 percent was Christian; 6.3 percent Hindu; 2.6 Confucian, Taoist, and other Chinese faiths; 0.8 percent practitioners of tribal and folk religions; and 0.4 percent adherents of other faiths. Another 0.8 percent professed no faith, and the religious affiliation of 0.4 percent was listed as unknown. Religious issues have been politically divisive, particularly as non-Muslims opposed attempts to institute Islamic law in states such as Terengganu in 2003.

Education and Literacy: From 1991 to 2000, the literacy rate for persons aged 10 to 64 years of age increased from 88.6 percent to 93.5 percent. Government-assisted schools provide free education for children between ages six and 18, but only primary education (ages six to 12) is compulsory. In 2003 Malaysia operated 7,498 primary schools and 1,916 secondary schools and also funded specialized schools for religious education and special education. Primary education starts at age six, secondary education at age 12, and students may attend vocational or technical schools in lieu of the final four years of secondary education. Private schools receive no government funds but are subject to government regulation.

Bahasa Malaysia is the principal language of instruction. Chinese and Tamil are used only in primary education. English is taught as a second language. In 1994 English-language instruction was introduced to promote multiethnic socialization and to improve science and mathematics education. By 2003 legislation required that all mathematics and science courses be taught in English. Educational policies frequently have contentious overtones, often because of perceived ethnic discrimination.

Health: Health indicators and infrastructure have improved substantially since independence. Increasing deaths from heart disease, cancer, and diabetes suggest increasing health problems associated with high-income countries, but the country is also still affected by health problems that are more common in low-income countries. In 2004 the most common communicable diseases were dengue fever, malaria, measles, and tuberculosis. Human immunodeficiency virus (HIV) was among common communicable diseases, but figures vary as to its prevalence. According to United Nations data, approximately 51,000 persons aged 15 to 49 had HIV in 2003, and the HIV prevalence rate was 0.4 percent, lower than the 0.6 percent rate for South and Southeast Asia overall.

These improvements are often attributed to improvements in public nutrition, sanitation, and access to health services. Health services at public hospitals are highly subsidized and free to persons who cannot afford the costs, but private expenditures account for more than half of total health spending. The Ministry of Health operates public health services, and from 2000 to 2004 the ministry's budget increased from approximately 6.3 percent to 8 percent of the national budget. In 2004 there were 1,969 public dental clinics, 1,924 rural clinics, 165 mobile clinics, 93 maternity and child health clinics, 125 government hospitals, and 218 private hospitals and "maternity/nursing homes." There were also 18,246 doctors, or one doctor for every 1,402 persons. Health services are more available in urban than in rural areas, but Malaysia has been developing "telehealth" and "telemedicine" for rural populations. In an effort to overcome a dearth of medical personnel, the government has built an "information technology-based" hospital in which patient data are stored in a central database rather than in paper files so that doctors can spend more time with patients than on paperwork.

Welfare: Observers often contend that the government has become very successful at managing social welfare and poverty reduction. Indeed, many development agencies have limited or ended their activities in Malaysia. The Department of Social Welfare administers 48 facilities that provide services for elderly persons, juvenile offenders, physically and mentally disabled persons, and others. The Social Security Organisation (SOCSO) administers social insurance, such as medical and disability benefits, for people—and their dependents—who are injured or killed in the course of employment. Available data suggest that from 1975 to 2002 the number of persons receiving social welfare services ranged from 4,000 to 6,000 persons annually, and that the number of persons receiving social insurance increased from 9,348 to 239,372. The Employee Provident Fund (EPF) provides retirement benefits derived from compulsory contributions from employees and the government. From 1975 to 2002, the number of employees who contributed to the EPF increased from 2.9 million to 10.2 million.

ECONOMY

Overview: Since the 1970s, Malaysia has transformed itself from an economy dependent on raw materials production and with a largely poor population to a multisector economy with a middle-income population. These changes have been most evident in Peninsular Malaysia, but there have also been significant changes in East Malaysia. The industrial sector has been the primary source of economic growth since the 1980s, particularly the manufacturing of electronics for export. However, export dependence has exposed the economy to global market fluctuations and to economic changes in its top export destinations and key sources of foreign investment, such as Japan and the United States. Both government and independent economists contend that private consumption has led to growth in the services sector and boosted economic growth overall. From 1997 to 2002, the country's economy declined for many reasons, but it has rebounded because of government policies such as fiscal stimulus packages, healthy foreign exchange reserves, low inflation, and low external debt.

Gross Domestic Product (GDP)/Power Purchasing Parity (PPP): Statistics vary but often suggest similar trends with GDP and PPP. According to the World Bank, from 1975 to 2004 the GDP (in current US$) grew from US$9.9 billion to US$118.3 billion, averaging 6.4 percent annual growth. Government figures put the 2005 GDP at US$130.1 billion. From 1975 to 2004, PPP (in current international dollars) grew from US$13.8 billion to US$255.8 billion, and GDP per capita expressed as PPP per capita (in current international dollars) grew from US$1,130 to US$9,630. According to the Malaysian government, the agricultural sector provided 8.7 percent of the GDP in 2005, industry provided 48.8 percent, and services provided 46.3 percent (these figures do not total 100 percent because import duties and imputed bank service charges are also factored into calculations of GDP by sector).

Government Budget: In fiscal year (FY) 2005, government revenues totaled US$30.6 billion, and expenditures were US$34.6 billion, including US$9.4 billion in capital expenditures. The government's budget deficit was estimated to be 3.8 percent of gross domestic product (GDP), down from 5.6 percent in FY2002. Public debt was 48.3 percent of GDP.

Inflation: According to World Bank figures, inflation (in terms of consumer prices) averaged nearly 3.6 percent annually from 1975 to 2004 but was 3.0 percent each year from 2000 to 2004. Since 2000 inflation has resulted largely from fiscal policies, such as reduced government subsidies for fuel and higher taxes on cigarettes and liquor.

Agriculture, Forestry, and Fishing: Agriculture, forestry, and fishing have not declined in terms of productive output but have declined as a proportion of economic output. From 1980 to 2005, the percentage of the gross domestic product (GDP) provided by agriculture declined from 22.6 percent to approximately 8.7 percent. In the same time period, the percentage of the total labor force employed in agriculture fell from 37.2 percent to approximately 13.1 percent. Despite these declines, Malaysia is the world's top producer of palm oil and is a major producer of bananas, cocoa, coconuts, pepper, pineapples, rice, rubber, and tea. In statistics, forestry and fishing often are categorized as agriculture. At one time, Malaysia was the world's largest exporter of tropical hardwoods, but sustainable management policies have reduced timber exports. Log production was 19.1 million cubic meters in 1975, peaked at 40.1 million cubic meters in 1990, and declined to 20.6 million cubic meters by 2002. Fishing accounted for 13.4 percent of the value of agricultural output in 2000 but declined to 11.8 percent by 2006; the government has invested in aquaculture to improve the output of the fishing industry.

Mining and Minerals: Malaysia is the world's leading tin producer and an important producer of other nonenergy minerals including bauxite, coal, copper, gold, and iron. However, mining has declined in its contribution to the economy and labor force. From 1980 to 2005, the percentage of the labor force employed in mining and quarrying fell from 1.6 percent to an estimated 0.4 percent, and as a percentage of gross domestic product mining and quarrying declined from 10.1 percent to 6.7 percent.

Industry and Manufacturing: The industrial sector arguably is Malaysia's most important economic sector, particularly the manufacturing subsector. According to government and World Bank data, from 1980 to 2005 the industrial sector's share of total employment increased from 24.1 percent to 36.1 percent, and its share of gross domestic product (GDP) increased from 41 percent to 48.8 percent in the same time period. When industry is disaggregated into subsectors, manufacturing's share of total employment increased from 15.7 percent to 28.4 percent, while mining and construction decreased from 8.4 percent to 7.7 percent of total employment in the same period. Furthermore, from 1980 to 2005 manufacturing increased from 21.5 percent of GDP to 31.5 percent, while mining and construction declined from 19.5 percent of GDP to 9.4 percent. High-technology exports have accounted for much of industrial growth. Other important industries are chemical products, light manufacturing, logging and timber processing, petroleum production and refining, and rubber and plastic products.

Energy: Energy production, consumption, and marketing have changed tremendously since the early 1970s. Historically, three state firms have dominated energy generation and distribution, but in 1994 the government allowed private producers into the market, and 15 independent producers were in operation by 2005. Still, all oil and gas resources are vested in state-owned Petroliam Nasional Berhad (Petronas). From 1971 to 2001, energy production increased from 4,770 kilotons of oil equivalent (KTOE) to 77,623 KTOE, as energy use increased from 6,032 KTOE to 51,608 KTOE. In the same period, oil sources fell from 72.4 percent of total electricity production to 8.6 percent, while natural gas increased from 0 percent to 78.1 percent. The remainder of electricity production in 2001 was provided by hydropower (9.9 percent) and coal (3.4 percent). Malaysia's proven oil reserves declined from a peak of 4.3 billion barrels in 1996 to 3.0 billion barrels in 2005, but the country has engaged in offshore development to increase oil production. Malaysia also has 75 trillion cubic feet of proven natural gas reserves, and liquefied natural gas production increased from 12.9 million tonnes in 1996 to 20.9 million tonnes in 2005, most of which is exported. In official statistics, employment in electricity and gas supply is combined with employment in water supply; from 1980 to 2005, these industries' share of total employment increased from 15.7 percent to approximately 28.4 percent.

Services: The services sector is very important in terms of its contribution to the country's gross domestic product (GDP) and overall employment. Service industries have grown primarily in response to industrial development but nevertheless are critical for the success of industry. According to government and World Bank data, the services sector increased from 36.3 percent of GDP in 1980 to 46.3 percent in 2005, and the proportion of the labor force employed in the services sector increased from 38.7 percent to 50.8 percent in the same period. In terms of value added, the most important service industries have been telecommunications, sea and air transport, hotels and other lodging, and financial services.

Banking and Finance: The 1997 financial crisis hurt banking, but since that time the National Asset Management Agency and the Corporate Debt Restructuring Committee have resolved numerous bad loans and debts. Indeed, nonperforming loans were reduced from 8 percent of total loans in 1998 to 4.4 percent by April 2006. The government has tried to improve corporate transparency by requiring publicly listed companies to submit quarterly reports. The Bank Negara Malaysia (BNM, Central Bank of Malaysia) has authority over the banking system and monetary policy, and the BNM's total assets grew from US$6.6 billion in 1985 to US$82.9 billion by April 2006. As of April 2006, there were 10 merchant banks with US$5.5 billion in fixed deposits and 31 commercial banks with total deposits of US$120.8 billion. In addition, banks following Islamic banking procedures had a total of US$17.6 billion in deposits in April 2006. As of 2004, 53 banks had offshore licenses in Labuan, off the cost of Sabah. The country has two stock exchanges, the Malaysia Derivatives Exchange (MDEX) and the Kuala Lumpur Stock Exchange (KLSE). In April 2006, the KLSE had 1,027 listed companies and a market capitalization of US$202.8 billion.

Tourism: Tourism is the second largest source of foreign exchange, and the industry has grown consistently with the exception of a brief lull after the terrorist attack in Bali, Indonesia, in October 2002. From 1990 to 2005, tourist arrivals increased from 7.4 million to 16.7 million; more than half the tourists were from Singapore. From 1990 to 2005, tourist receipts increased from US$1.7 billion to US$8.4 billion per year. In 2003 the government announced the establishment of a US$105.3 million Special Tourism Fund to revive the tourism industry and a US$52.6 million Tourist Infrastructure Fund to build and upgrade tourist facilities and amenities.

Labor: In 2005 the labor force participation rate was 66 percent of all persons aged 15 to 64 but higher for males (85.2 percent) than for females (45.8 percent). From 1980 to 2005, the labor force increased from 5.1 million to 10.9 million people. In the same time period, the official unemployment rate ranged from 3 percent to 8 percent; it was 3.5 percent in 2005. In 2005 the majority of the labor force worked in the industrial and services sectors (36.1 percent and 50.8 percent, respectively) and the rest in the agricultural sector. In 2005 Malaysia had 617 trade unions with a total membership of 801,000. Legally, the normal workweek may not exceed 48 hours, overtime pay is 1.5 times the hourly rate of pay, female employees receive 60 consecutive days of maternity leave, and, even with no general minimum wage, the government can designate minimum wages for particular industries.

Foreign Economic Relations: Malaysia has been a member of the World Trade Organization since January 1, 1995. Major trading partners include China, Japan, and the United States, although Malaysia has pursued bilateral free-trade agreements with Australia, India, New

Zealand, Pakistan, and South Korea. Malaysia also has participated in regional free-trade and investment relations with many of the same countries through the Association of South East Asian Nations (ASEAN). The government's only major trade dispute has been an objection to the U.S decision to ban imports of shrimp and shrimp products from Malaysia and other countries. This dispute commenced in 1996 and continued into 2006.

Imports: Malaysia's imports of goods and services (in current U.S. dollars) grew steadily from US$938.4 million in 1960 to US$114.5 billion in 2005. Major imports include machinery and transport equipment, basic manufactures, and mineral products. The principal import sources have been Japan (15.9 percent of total imports in 2004), the United States (14.5 percent), and Singapore (11.1 percent). Other important sources have included China, Taiwan, and Thailand.

Exports: Exports of goods and services (in current U.S. dollars) grew from US$1.2 billion in 1960 to US$140.8 billion in 2005. Major exports include chemicals, liquefied natural gas, petroleum products, electrical machinery and parts, and particularly electronic equipment and semiconductors. The principal export markets have been the United States, Singapore, and Japan. International investors believe Malaysia' currency is undervalued, and this has improved the competitiveness of Malaysian exports.

Trade Balance: According to World Bank and government data, Malaysia experienced both trade deficits and surpluses from 1960 to 1995 but only surpluses from 1996 to 2005, largely as a result of growth in exports of electrical and electronic goods. The external balance on goods and services was US$1.4 billion (in current U.S. dollars) in fiscal year (FY) 1996 and US$26.3 billion in FY 2005.

Balance of Payments: According to World Bank and government figures, prior to 1998 current account balances registered both surpluses and deficits, demonstrating no clear trend toward one or the other. However, Malaysia had a current account surplus from 1998 to 2005 that amounted to US$19.3 billion in fiscal year (FY) 2005. The improvement has been attributed to several factors, including higher trade balances and inflows of foreign direct investment into manufacturing and services.

External Debt: According to government data, from 1980 to 2005 the government's external debt increased from US$2.2 billion to US$8.3 billion but declined from 10.9 percent of gross domestic product (GDP) to 6.5 percent of GDP. Total debt to multilateral lenders increased from US$593 million in 1980 to US$1.1 billion in 1991, declining thereafter to US$968.9 million in 2005. However, the government's portion of total external debt is quite small: 16.1 percent in 2005, compared with 30.5 percent for nonfinancial public enterprises (such as Petronas) and 53.4 percent for the private sector.

Foreign Investment: Foreign direct investment (FDI) increased from US$350.5 million in 1975 to US$5.2 billion in 1992, declined to US$287.1 million by 2001, and increased to US$4.6 billion in 2004, the last year for which figures are publicly available. Generally, most FDI has come from Japan, Singapore, the United Kingdom, and the United States. The government has expressed concern that Malaysia's competitiveness in attracting FDI may be hindered by various factors, including wages that are higher than those in other Asian countries, and has liberalized foreign investment policies to attract FDI, particularly in biotechnology, high-technology manufacturing, and tourism.

Foreign Aid: From 1960 to 2004 (the most recent year for which data are available), official development aid to Malaysia increased from US$12.8 million to US$289.5 million per year—an increase from US$1.56 per capita in 1960 to US$11.49 per capita in 2004. Approximately 99 percent of official development aid in 2004 was bilateral aid, and nearly all of that came from Japan.

Currency and Exchange Rate: The official currency is the ringgit (MYR), which is subdivided into 100 sen. The August 2006 average exchange rate was MYR3.67/US$1. In 2005 the average exchange rate was MYR3.79 to US$1, but from October 1, 1997, to July 21, 2005, the government fixed the ringgit's value at MYR3.80 to US$1 and made it nonconvertible in other countries. The government created these controls after the 1997 Asian economic crisis in order to limit economic exposure to regional economic changes and to stabilize domestic prices and exchange rates. The government reportedly lifted these controls to make the currency competitive with the Chinese yuan, which China revalued in July 2005.

Fiscal Year: Malaysia's fiscal year runs from October 1 through September 30.

TRANSPORTATION AND TELECOMMUNICATIONS

Overview: Malaysia has very modern transportation and telecommunications infrastructures, but their quality and availability vary geographically. In much of the country, mountainous terrain has limited transportation infrastructure development, and sufficient government funding to overcome such constraints only began to materialize in the 1980s. Prime Minister Abdullah Ahmad Badawi (elected in 2003) has proved more financially conservative with transportation programs than his predecessor, Mahathir Mohamad, whose transportation programs have been criticized as grandiose and costly. Government road-building programs have responded ambitiously to increased private car ownership, but the rail system has changed little since colonial times, with the major exception of Kuala Lumpur's commuter rail system. Roads and rail lines are concentrated on the peninsula, particularly in populous areas west of the mountains. In East Malaysia, rail service is minimal; roads provide all-weather access among major towns but are rudimentary elsewhere. The Ministry of Transport's total estimated expenditures were US$400.1 million in fiscal year (FY) 2006, down from US$685 million in FY 2005, or 1.1 percent of total government expenditures in FY2006, also down from 2.2 percent in FY2005.

Malaysia's telecommunications network is among the most modern in Asia. Since the 1980s when the government liberalized telecommunications policies, the country has pursued ambitious programs to place itself prominently in global telecommunications. In 1996 the government established a Multimedia Super Corridor (MSC) as an international center for information communication technology companies to develop and export products. The government's promotion of telecommunications also has improved governance in some ways, such as adding transparency to government procedures and increasing access to politicians, bureaucrats, and policy information. The government also has deregulated and liberalized

16

investment in the telecommunications industry and, to a lesser extent, allowable content. Foreign entities are allowed to own up to 30 percent of local communications companies. Several ministries and departments administer telecommunications; thus, telecommunications expenditures are broadly distributed and not given a specific expenditure in the federal budget.

Roads: From 1995 to 2005, total road length increased from 61,380 kilometers to 77,673 kilometers. Most roads (67.7 percent) are in Peninsular Malaysia, but the government has increased funding for roads in East Malaysia. The private sector was heavily involved in road building until the 1997 economic crisis, and the government funded completion of some major projects. Still, many new roads are tolled and administered by companies with government links. In 2005 there were 6.5 million registered automobiles, 7 million registered motorcycles, and approximately 1.3 million other registered vehicles, including taxis and buses; nearly 90 percent were registered in Peninsular Malaysia.

Railroads: Malaysia's rail system has changed little since independence, largely because of difficult terrain and poor funding. The sole rail freight operator is government-owned Keretapi Tanah Melayu Berhad (KTMB), which is operated on a cost-recovery basis. In 2004 KTMB had 164 locomotives, 190 passenger coaches, and 3,509 freight wagons. In 2006 there were 2,262 kilometers of rail lines, including 2,128 kilometers in Peninsular Malaysia. The peninsula has two main rail lines, both of which link to the State Railway of Thailand: a 787-kilometer line between Singapore and Butterworth and a 528-kilometer line along the east coast. Rail gauge and electrification data vary, but about 90 percent of rail lines are 1.000-meter gauge, and fewer than 10 percent are electrified. The only commuter rail system is in Kuala Lumpur; it is composed of five separately managed rail services, including a monorail, an automated line, and a 160-kilometer-per-hour express line that serves Kuala Lumpur International Airport. From 1997 to 2005, the system's average daily ridership grew from nearly 47,000 to 433,000.

Ports: Ports are an important element of Malaysia's foreign trade-dependent economy. Since the early 1990s, the government has undertaken many projects to improve port operations and enlarge capacity in all 93 ports. The Ministry of Transportation administers seven "federal" ports, all privatized except Kemaman. The states of Sabah and Sarawak administer 16 "state" ports, and the Marine Department manages 70 "minor" ports, including one private port (Teluk Ewa). The ports with the highest cargo volumes are Bintulu, Pasir Gudang (Johor), Port Dickson, Pulau Pinang (Penang), Sabah, and Port Klang (Kelang), the nation's designated transshipment port. From 1996 to 2005, the amount of cargo handled by larger ports grew from 152.3 million tonnes to 369.4 million tonnes, and containerized cargo increased from 2.1 million twenty-foot-equivalent-units (TEUs) to 12.1 million TEUs.

Inland and Coastal Waterways: In 2004 Malaysia had approximately 7,200 kilometers of waterways: 3,200 kilometers in Peninsular Malaysia, 1,500 kilometers in Sabah, and 2,500 kilometers in Sarawak. Rivers and tributaries are of only marginal significance on the peninsula, but they are a major means of transportation in Sabah and Sarawak. As a result of high, year-round precipitation, rivers never run dry and are nearly always navigable, although silting often limits navigation to canoes and rafts.

Civil Aviation and Airports: In 2004 Malaysia had 117 airports, 37 of which had paved runways, and one heliport. The main airports that service international flights are Kota Kinabalu, Kuala Lumpur, Kuching, Langkawi, Pulau Pinang (Penang), and Senai (also called Sultan Ismail Airport). The national airline, Malaysia Airline System Berhad (or Malaysian Airlines), was privatized in 1985, but financial difficulties have threatened its solvency since 2001. The company operated 100 aircraft in 2004. Malaysia also has three regional airlines, one charter airline, and one helicopter company, Sabah Air. From 1995 to 2005, air passenger traffic increased from 27.3 million to 42.8 million passengers per year, and cargo handled increased from 482,030 tonnes to 1,006,814 tonnes.

Pipelines: In 2004 Malaysia had 7,281 kilometers of pipelines: 5,047 kilometers for gas, 1,841 kilometers for oil, 279 kilometers for condensate, and 114 kilometers for refined products.

Telecommunications: Malaysia's telecommunications infrastructure is generally regarded as on par with that of Western countries but is largely concentrated in urban areas. Telekom Malaysia Berhad (TM) is the sole provider of landline telephones, and the government owns the majority of TM's shares. The telephone system provides good service internationally and among urban areas. In 2003 there were an estimated 4.6 million fixed telephone lines. In 2002 there were an estimated 11.1 million mobile telephone users. Four operators dominate the telecommunications market, which accounts for 62 percent of industry revenue. In 2004 Malaysia had 170 personal computers per 1,000 persons and an estimated 8.7 million Internet users (in 2003). The government has established the Multimedia Super Corridor (MSC) near Kuala Lumpur in an effort to become the global center for information communication technology.

GOVERNMENT AND POLITICS

Government Overview: Malaysia is a federated constitutional monarchy based on a parliamentary system of government and an independent judiciary. States in Malaysia have their own constitutions and governments. Political institutions continue to evolve for many reasons, including recent emergence from colonialism, greater focus on economic rather than political development, and coexisting traditional and nontraditional authorities. Indeed, the supreme institution is the Conference of Rulers (Majilis Raja-Raja), which is composed of the hereditary rulers of nine states in Peninsular Malaysia and four state governors appointed by the king. The nine hereditary rulers in the Conference of Rulers elect one of themselves as the "supreme sovereign" or king (Yang di-Pertuan Agong) who acts as head of state for a single five-year term. The deputy head of state is elected in the same manner and, although exercising no power, is available to fill the king's position if the latter is absent or disabled. Technically, all government acts are legitimized by the king's authority, and the civilian and military public services officially owe their loyalty to the king and hereditary rulers. However, the king only acts on the advice of both parliament and the cabinet, and in practice the prime minister is the most powerful political authority.

From 1981 to 2003, Prime Minister Mahathir Mohamed was unquestionably the most powerful and influential political figure in Malaysia, substantially influencing economic and social development. His successor, Abdullah Ahmad Badawi, has focused on reducing public spending, deferring several large-scale infrastructure projects, and promoting agricultural and educational development. Since the 1960s, the same political coalition, led by Mahathir and Abdullah's political party, has governed the country. Some observers contend that corruption is problematic in politics, but international organizations that focus on corruption generally suggest that while Malaysian politics and business exhibit a degree of corruption, Malaysia has less corruption than most countries in the world.

Executive Branch: Malaysia has several bodies that can exercise executive power. The Conference of Rulers (Majlis Raja-Raja) is the supreme institution that is constitutionally empowered to select the king (Yang di-Pertuan Agong), approve appointed judges, rule on administrative policy changes, and deliberate on national policy questions. The king is the head of state and supreme commander of the armed forces, and he may authorize requests to dissolve parliament and approve parliamentary bills. However, the king actually has limited executive powers and may act only under the advice of the prime minister and cabinet. The prime minister, leader of the party that holds a plurality of seats in the House of Representatives (lower house of parliament), is the head of government and exercises most executive power. The prime minister appoints cabinet members with the king's consent.

Legislative Branch: The legislature consists of the king and a bicameral parliament with an upper house (Senate, or Dewan Negara) and a lower house (House of Representatives, or Dewan Rakyat). The Senate is a permanent body consisting of 70 members that serve three-year terms; each of the 13 State Legislative Assemblies elects two members; and the king appoints 44 members, four of whom are from the federal territories of Kuala Lumpur (2), Labuan, and Putrajaya. The Senate elects its president and deputy president from among its own members. The House of Representatives consists of 219 members who are popularly elected for five years from single-member constituencies. The Senate may initiate legislation, but only the House of Representatives can initiate legislation that involves the granting of funds. Both houses of parliament and the king must approve legislation for it to be enacted into law. The king has few other legislative powers, but he may dissolve the House of Representatives on the prime minister's advice.

Judicial Branch: Malaysia has an independent judiciary and two court systems. The sharia system, which issues rulings under Islamic law, is composed of a high court and courts in each state. A system of superior and subordinate courts handles civil and criminal law. Superior courts include the Federal Court, the Court of Appeals, and two High Courts. The Federal Court is the highest judicial authority and final court of appeal. It has original, referral, and advisory jurisdiction as well as jurisdiction over disputes involving states and the federal government. The Federal Court has a chief justice and 10 judges; the number of judges needed for rulings varies according to the type of case. The Court of Appeals acts as an appeals court between the Federal Court and the High Courts. The High Courts—one each for eastern and western Malaysia—have original, appellate, and revisionary jurisdiction. A Special Court hears civil and criminal cases involving state rulers and the supreme ruler. The attorney general, as the principal legal officer and public prosecutor, provides legal advice to the executive branch and may draft bills for deliberation and enactment by parliament.

Subordinate courts include 60 sessions courts, 151 magistrate courts, and the Court for Children, which hears juvenile cases. Subordinate courts have jurisdiction over criminal cases not subject to the death penalty. Sessions courts can hear civil cases valued up to US$65,693, and magistrate courts have jurisdiction over civil cases valued up to US$6,596. Native courts in Sabah and Sarawak and *penghulu* (village headman) courts in the peninsula handle misdemeanors and civil disputes according to traditional customs, but under state jurisdiction.

Administrative Divisions: Malaysia is a federation of 13 states and three federal territories. The states are Johor, Kedah, Kelantan, Melaka, Negeri Sembilan, Pahang, Perak, Perlis, Pulau Pinang, Sabah, Sarawak, Selangor, and Terengganu. The federal territories are Kuala Lumpur, Labuan, and Putrajaya. Peninsular states are divided into a total of 137 administrative districts, Sabah is divided into four residences, and Sarawak is divided into five residences.

Provincial and Local Government: The Ministry of Federal Territories administers federal territories, but states have their own governments and constitutions. State governments are composed of a legislative assembly, a speaker of the house, and a head of state. Legislative assembly members are elected by single-member constituencies, and assembly members in turn elect the speaker. Legislative assemblies may make or enact laws not reserved for the federal legislature and on subjects under the concurrent purview of federal and state governments. Heads of state are hereditary rulers, except in Melaka, Pulau Pinang, Sabah, and Sarawak, which have governors appointed by the king upon the chief minister's advice. The head of state appoints a chief minister from among legislative members, may dissolve assemblies on the chief minister's advice, and must approve all legislation. The head of state is the chief executive, subject to advice from an executive council headed by the chief minister. However, chief ministers actually handle state administrative matters, assisted by a cabinet of ministers. State-level agencies enforce and administer state laws, just as federal agencies do for federal laws. District and municipal councils handle policy matters at those respective levels.

Judicial and Legal System: The federal constitution of Malaysia is the supreme law of the land, and the legal system is based on English common law. The judiciary is a newly established and evolving institution. Until 1985 the highest court of appeal was the Privy Court, located in the United Kingdom. Malaysia has a death penalty and no trial by jury. Critics and jurists contend that the system is beset by many problems, such as case backlogs, corruption, poor legal representation, and a changing institutional structure.

Electoral System: Malaysia has universal suffrage for citizens 21 years of age and older.

Politics and Political Parties: Since independence, Malaysia has been governed by a coalition of political parties called the National Front (Barisan Nasional—BN), which consisted of 14 political parties in the 2004 elections. The United Malays National Organisation (UMNO) has been the dominant party in both the BN and the country. The Malaysian Chinese Association (MCA) and the Malaysian Indian Congress (MIC; formerly the Malayan Indian Congress) have also been influential in the BN. Significant opposition parties include the Pan Malaysian Islamic Party (Parti Islam Se-Malaysia—PAS) and the People's Justice Party (Parti Keadilan Rakyat—Keadilan). Political parties often draw much of their support from distinct ethnic or religious communities, and their electoral success appears to rely on an individual leader's influence.

Political parties often are characterized by factionalism, publicized internal disputes, and near cloak-and-dagger internal relations. As the perennial majority party in the BN, the UMNO has also created barriers for parties to compete in elections, such as increasing the amount of required deposits.

Measured by the number of seats in the 2004 elections for the House of Representatives, the most supported political party was the UMNO, which won 109 of the 219 seats, followed by the MCA (31 seats), Democratic Action Party (12 seats), Parti Pesakea Bumiputera Bersatu (11 seats), and Parti Gerakan Rakyat Malaysia (10 seats). All other political parties won fewer than 10 seats. The BN coalition won 198 out of 219 seats in the 2004 elections. In the 12 general elections since 1955, the BN and its predecessor, the Alliance, have won at least 70 percent of seats, except in 1969 when they won only 51 percent of seats.

Mass Media: Mass media are often discussed in terms of the substantial legal restrictions on acceptable content rather than the increased availability of media. The 1998 Communications and Multimedia Act liberalized acceptable broadcast content and made broadcasters responsible for regulating their own content within legal parameters. The Ministry of Energy, Water, and Communications and the Communications and Multimedia Commission regulate electronic and print media and may revoke the license of any company that is deemed to have violated acceptable media content. The constitution protects freedom of the press, but critics contend that legal parameters on content are highly restrictive and politically motivated.

Government-owned Radio Televisyen Malaysia (RTM), the predominant broadcaster, operates nine national radio services and 16 regional radio services. The government also owns Institut Kefahaman Islam Malaysia, a religious radio broadcaster. The Voice of Malaysia (VOM) is the government's international radio service. Malaysia also has seven commercial radio broadcasters and two university radio stations. In 2001 there were 35 AM radio stations, 391 FM radio stations, and 15 shortwave radio stations. RTM has two national television services, and three commercial broadcasters serve only the peninsula. The Malaysian National News Agency (Bernama) is the official news agency and has exclusive rights to receive and distribute news in Malaysia. In 2000, Malaysia had 31 daily newspapers with a total average circulation of 2.2 million.

Foreign Relations: During the Cold War, Malaysia's foreign policy was directed toward defeating domestic insurgency and constraining international communism. Since the defeat of the insurgency in 1989 and the later decline of socialist governments, Malaysia's foreign relations have been largely characterized by economic and trade issues and by its domestic treatment of immigrants. Relations with many Asian countries have improved as a result of growing trade, but Chinese, Indonesian, and Philippine authorities have expressed concern about official and societal treatment of fellow ethnics within Malaysia. The United States regards Malaysia as having undertaken important steps against terrorism, such as creating a counterterrorism training center, but Malaysian authorities have been upset by the U.S. listing of Malaysia as a "terror-risk" country. Relations with the Philippines also have been strained over allegations that members of the Moro Islamic Liberation Front, a Filipino insurgent group, have commandeered parts of Borneo as a haven. Relations with Brunei and Singapore have been tense because of disputed territorial claims that involve commercial and natural resource interests.

Membership in International Organizations: Malaysia is a member of numerous international organizations including the Asian Development Bank; Asia-Pacific Economic Cooperation; Association of South East Asian Nations; Bank for International Settlements; Colombo Plan; Commonwealth; East Asia Summit; Food and Agriculture Organization of the United Nations; Group of 15; Group of 77; International Atomic Energy Agency; International Bank for Reconstruction and Development; International Centre for Settlement of Investment Disputes; International Chamber of Commerce; International Civil Aviation Organization; International Confederation of Free Trade Unions; International Criminal Police Organization; International Development Association; International Development Bank; International Federation of Red Cross and Red Crescent Societies; International Finance Corporation; International Fund for Agricultural Development; International Hydrographic Organization; International Labour Organization; International Maritime Organization; International Monetary Fund; International Olympic Committee; International Organization for Standardization; International Telecommunication Union; Inter-Parliamentary Union; Multilateral Investment Guarantee Association; Nonaligned Movement; Organisation for the Prohibition of Chemical Weapons; Organization of the Islamic Conference; Permanent Court of Arbitration; United Nations (UN); UN Educational, Scientific and Cultural Organization; UN Industrial Development Organization; Universal Postal Union; World Bank; World Confederation of Labor; World Customs Organization; World Federation of Trade Unions; World Health Organization; World Intellectual Property Organization; World Meteorological Organization; World Tourism Organization; and World Trade Organization.

Major International Treaties: Malaysia is a signatory to numerous international treaties including the Basel Convention on the Control of Transboundary Movements of Hazardous Wastes and Their Disposal; Chemical Weapons Convention; Comprehensive Nuclear Test Ban Treaty (signed but not ratified as of July 2006); Convention on Biological Diversity; Convention on Fishing and Conservation of Living Resources of the High Seas; Convention on International Trade in Endangered Species of Wild Flora and Fauna; Convention on the Elimination of All Forms of Discrimination Against Women; Convention on the Rights of the Child; Convention on Wetlands of International Importance Especially as Waterfowl Habitat; Geneva Protocol; International Tropical Timber Agreement 1983; International Tropical Timber Agreement 1994; Kyoto Protocol to the United Nations Framework Convention on Climate Change; Montreal Protocol on Substances that Deplete the Ozone layer; Protocol of 1978 Relating to the International Convention for the Prevention of Pollution from Ships, 1973; Treaty Banning Nuclear Weapon Tests in the Atmosphere, in Outer Space, and Under Water; Treaty on the Non-Proliferation of Nuclear Weapons; United Nations Convention to Combat Desertification; United Nations Convention on the Law of the Sea; and United Nations Framework Convention on Climate Change.

NATIONAL SECURITY

Armed Forces Overview: Malaysia has three military services—the army, navy, and air force. Foreign observers estimate that in 2005 active-duty armed forces personnel totaled 110,000: 80,000 in the Malaysian Army (Tentera Darat Malaysia), 15,000 in the Royal Malaysian Navy (Tentera Laut Diraja Malaysia), and 15,000 in the Royal Malaysian Air Force (Tentera Udara

Diraja Malaysia,). There were also 51,600 reserves—50,000 in the army, 1,000 in the navy, and 600 in the air force. Historically, security threats have been largely internal. Thus, the country's military is primarily organized to address internal security matters and is strongly oriented toward infantry. The government also has attempted to address internal security through emphasizing ethnic harmony and economic growth.

Malaysia's geography poses inherent security problems and benefits. The physical separation of Peninsular Malaysia and East Malaysia by the South China Sea, numerous shared borders, and an extensive coast create obstacles for securing the country. However, the peninsula's position on one of the world's busiest sea lanes, the Strait of Malacca, also means that numerous countries are economically interdependent with Malaysia and thus invested in its national security and stability.

Foreign Military Relations: In terms of multilateral military relations, Malaysia has a common defense agreement with other nations in the Association of South East Asian Nations (ASEAN) and is a member of the Five Power Defence Agreement with Australia, New Zealand, Singapore, and the United Kingdom. In regard to bilateral military relations, Malaysia allows the United States to use naval and air repair and maintenance facilities in Malaysia.

External Threat: Malaysia has no immediate external security threats. The country does have territorial disputes with other countries, but none has resulted in a militarized dispute since the 1960s or is expected to do so in the near future.

Defense Budget: From fiscal year (FY) 2002 to FY2004, Malaysia's defense budget increased from US$2.2 billion to US$2.2 billion but decreased from 2.3 percent of gross domestic product (GDP) in 2002 to 1.9 percent of GDP in 2004. In the same period, foreign military assistance increased 50 percent from US$800,000 to US$1.2 million.

Major Military Units: The army consists of two military regions, one headquarters field command, and four area commands. In addition, the army has one mechanized infantry brigade, 11 infantry brigades, and one airborne brigade. The army's combat units include five armored regiments, 28 infantry battalions, three mechanized infantry battalions, three airborne battalions, five engineering regiments, one helicopter squadron, and one special forces regiment. The army's reserves are officially called the Territorial Army, consisting of 16 infantry regiments and five highway security battalions. The navy is organized into two commands: Naval Area 1 for the peninsula and Naval Area 2 for Sabah and Sarawak. The navy also has an aviation wing and a naval commando unit. The air force is organized into one air operations headquarters, two air divisions, one training and logistics command, and the Integrated Air Defence Systems Headquarters. The air force has three ground attack squadrons, two fighter squadrons, one reconnaissance squadron, one maritime reconnaissance squadron, and four transport squadrons.

Major Military Equipment: In 2005 the army was believed to have 26 light tanks, 186 reconnaissance vehicles, 111 armored personnel carriers, 130 105-millimeter towed artillery, 34 155-millimeter towed artillery, 232 81-millimeter mortars, 18 multiple rocket launchers, 60 antitank guided weapons, 584 rocket launchers, 260 recoilless launchers, 60 air defense guns, 48 surface-to-air missiles, 9 helicopters, and 165 assault craft. The navy has 4 frigates, 41 patrol and coastal combat vessels, 4 mine warfare vessels, 1 amphibious vessel, 4 support vessels, and 6 armed helicopters. The air force inventory includes 73 combat aircraft, 59 fighter and ground attack aircraft, 19 reconnaissance aircraft, 35 transport aircraft, 40 transport and search-and-rescue helicopters, 3 reconnaissance unmanned aerial vehicles, 20 training aircraft, and 13 training helicopters. The air force also has air-to-air and air-to-surface missiles, although the number is publicly unavailable. Since the mid-1990s, the countries that have provided the most military hardware to Malaysia have been France, New Zealand, Poland, Russia, and the United Kingdom.

Military Service: The minimum age for voluntary military service is 18. Women can serve in the military but only in noncombat positions. Malaysia's only form of conscription is the National Service Program, which requires three months of military service for approximately 80,000 18-year-old men and women randomly selected from the population. The program was established in February 2004 to improve the military and to promote national integration and patriotism. However, the program has been revamped to address problems such as its poor organization and ethnic divisions among recruits.

Paramilitary Forces: Malaysia has numerous paramilitary organizations, but estimates of their total personnel vary. Malaysian paramilitary forces include the General Operational Force with approximately 10,000 personnel, the marine police with 2,100 personnel, the police air unit whose personnel numbers are publicly unavailable, and area security units—an auxiliary force of the General Operations Force—with 35,000 personnel. In addition, there are 1,200 border scouts (in Sabah and Sarawak) and the People's Volunteer Corps, which has approximately 300,000 members and is involved in domestic security and community development projects.

Foreign Military Forces: Australia has 148 military personnel in Butterworth, Malaysia, as part of an ongoing commitment to the Five-Power Defence Agreement.

Military Forces Abroad: As of 2006, Malaysian troops were serving in United Nations (UN) peacekeeping operations in the Democratic Republic of the Congo, East Timor, Eritrea and Ethiopia, Liberia, Serbia and Montenegro, Sierra Leone, and Western Sahara. Malaysian troops previously have served on other UN peacekeeping missions.

Police: Malaysia's federal police force is the Royal Malaysian Police (RMP), which is under the direction of the Ministry of Home Affairs (MHA). States have their own police forces, which are subordinate to the RMP. Data on police are scant, but in 2000 the RMP had 82,383 total personnel, or 353.6 police for every 100,000 persons. In the same year, there were 167,173 total crimes (717.5 crimes per 100,000 persons), mostly thefts and burglaries. Most RMP personnel are Malay; females made up 9.7 percent of total personnel in 2000. The public often perceives the police as excessively forceful, repressive, and unprofessional. International observers contend that Malaysia's police force is among the country's most corrupt institutions, and a 2006 MHA report criticized the police for human rights violations, poor policing, and corruption.

Internal Security and Terrorism: Some observers regard religious fundamentalism as a potential danger to Malaysia's domestic security while others argue that religious extremism has been on the wane since 2001. Both the Malaysian government and outside observers contend that there is little terrorist activity in Malaysia but that the country is used as a haven for terrorists from neighboring countries. The government has forcefully cracked down on suspected terrorists and has developed high levels of counterterrorism capability and cooperation with Western governments. However, at least two notable militant groups are believed to have been active in Malaysia since the mid-1990s: the Kumplulan Mujahideen Malaysia (KMM) and Jemaah Islamiyah (JI), which is believed to be active in several countries in Southeast Asia. These two groups are allegedly linked, and the JI is believed to have links to al Qaeda. In 2001 the KMM was found to have possible links with the Pan Malaysian Islamic Party. Malaysian police have allegedly demolished another Islamic militant group called Federal Special Forces of Malaysia (Pasukan Khas Persekutuan Malaysia—PKPM,). Most extremist activity has occurred in the states of Johor, Kedah, Perlis, and Selangor, all on the western side of Peninsular Malaysia.

Malaysia has also experienced periodic protests and riots, for several reasons. Governmental limits on freedom of expression and political participation have contributed to such events. Perhaps even more troubling is that after these events there has been some evidence of increased ethnic divisiveness, including a rise in support for political parties with specific ethnic or religious constituencies. However, other evidence suggests that Malaysia has managed ethnic differences better than other pluralistic societies in Asia.

Human Rights: International and domestic human rights organizations and foreign governments are critical of the Malaysian government and in particular the Royal Malaysian Police (RMP), but human rights groups and foreign governments generally do not regard Malaysia as being among the world's worst abusers of human rights. International human rights groups have publicly expressed concern that preventive detention laws such as the Internal Security Act 1960 (ISA) and the Emergency (Public Order and Prevention of Crime) Ordinance 1969 allow for abuses such as detention without trial or charge. Moreover, human rights groups have documented severe abuse of prisoners. At least 112 people were detained under the ISA, and most were alleged to be Islamic militants, counterfeiters, and practitioners of religious faiths deemed deviant by the government. Critics also contend that the ruling United Malays National Organisation (UMNO) has used the ISA to detain an estimated 10,000 dissenters since 1960. Human rights organizations also insist that migrant workers are regularly abused, and indeed migrant workers are excluded from many provisions of Malaysian employment law. The RMP has been particularly criticized for unlawful killings, torture, and arbitrary arrests and detentions, although the Human Rights Commission of Malaysia was established in 1999. In addition, human rights groups affirm the presence of quotidian violence and oppression against women and children, including human trafficking.